My Grandpa is My Hero Too

This book is dedicated to my Grandpa, the late Roosevelt Stanley, and to all the loving Grandpas, Granddads, Pops, Paps, Poppas, Poppies, Paw-Paws, Big Daddies, Grand Dudes, Gramps, Abuelos, and Grandfathers who enrich the lives of their grandchildren every day.

LIFE LINES
LEGACY

Author's Foreword for Adults: The inspiration behind this book.

I loved my grandpa dearly. As a child, summers with him and grandma were full of joy — riding in the back of his old truck with my sisters and brothers, picking berries, playing with cousins, and soaking in the breeze on country roads.

I loved hearing him talk, telling stories and jokes that I still remember today.

Grandpa was a tall, slightly bowlegged man with a gentle spirit and a regal presence. He loved his family fiercely — his children, grandchildren, nieces, nephews, and especially Grandma. Their rustic country home, with no running water and no indoor bathroom, overflowed with peace, laughter, and love.

I admired his devotion to family, his stories, his hound dogs and chickens, and the way he preached — leaning back, hand to ear, ending with a whoop that made me proud to say, "That's my grandpa."

This book is a mosaic of his life. It is a tribute to his love, his lessons, and the legacy he passed down to my father who carried that same love into the next generation.

My grandpa looks like my dad,

and he is my hero too.

He lets me wear his jersey and hat,

gave me his special glove and bat.

He lets me pretend to drive his truck after we feed the hogs, chickens, and ducks.

He takes me everywhere he goes—
rubs my head and tickles my toes.

My grandpa loves me, and I love him too.

We spend so much time together, and we have a lot to do.

Whenever grandma gives him a 'honey-do' list,

He completes all his work, then she gives him a kiss.

Then we are free to have fun

for the rest of the day.

I love spending summers with them. I wish I could stay.

My grandpa's voice is deep, raspy, and kind.

"Quiet," he whispers as I throw my line.

We paddle our boat to the middle of the lake.

He keeps me calm when I see a snake.

"Don't worry, it won't hurt you,"

he says,

"Just stay still and calm."

Then my grandpa picks me up

and carries me in his arms.

Everyone in the community
knows my grandpa by name.
**He gives respect to everyone
and treats everyone the same.**

He works hard every day—
building houses, gardens, and toys.
There is nothing he can't do—
he does what he enjoys.

My grandpa showed my father how to build gardens and plant trees.
He loved the outdoors, and my father taught me.

My grandpa helps feed people in need.

He mentors young people and teaches them to succeed.

Whenever he sees someone in distress, he stops to help **— he gives his best.**

Whenever we go to the barber shop,
everybody there calls him "Pop."

He tips the barber who cuts his hair,
then tips the people working there.

He takes the team on the bus to the
game, then takes us all for a ride
on the train.

For all the service he gives everyday—
mentoring and volunteering in every way,
he has received awards and honors too.
I said, "Grandpa, I am so proud of you."

My grandpa tells great stories that make me proud.

He takes me to our family reunions.
Wow— what a crowd!

Lots of hugs, lots of love, as everyone is happy to see

our big, beautiful family.

Our family reunions are filled with fun.

We play games, swim, dance and run.

We sit and eat our aunties' good dishes,

Then gather 'round to share our stories and wishes.

Capturing Memories

Welcome to the Family Reunion

My grandparents loved their family — to see their children and grandchildren carry their legacy,

to grow up proud and strong,

and to know that family is where we belong.

My Grandpa wants me to know

our history, the brilliance of our legacy,

and all the injustices we overcame,
and how he marched peacefully
to help bring change.

He took me and my cousins

to the voting booth

so that we could see,

our right to choose in a democracy.

Standing between history and hope,

Grandpa showed us

how far we have come—
and how far we can go.

My grandpa took us to California to attend the graduation of Cousin Gwen. Like my uncle, she wants to be a vet — taking care of animals and pets.

He encourages us to get an education, go to tech school or join the armed forces if we want to serve the nation.

He said, "Whatever you do, do the best you can.
**"You are brilliant young ladies,
You are competent young men."**

My grandpa loves music too.
He plays the guitar and drums.
People come to hear him play
at the Center and the Red Barn.

At the center there is dancing, singing, and clapping.

Some of the children are even rapping.

The drums are beating, the tambourines slapping and

Grandpa's feet are stomping and tapping. Oh yeah!

My grandpa dresses up in a nice suit
and tie.

He said, "I am going to church.

Do you want to come?"

When I asked him why.

We went to church

and sang a lot of good songs.

Then Grandpa got up to preach.

The people said, "Amen" to his words,

Then he stretched his arms to reach.

He prayed for the people, and he prayed for me too.

And I hugged him and said,

"Grandpa you are my hero,

and I want to be like you."

Grandpa scraped the sweet gum trees, letting the resin drip in the summer breeze.

He picked sweet berries for us to share.

He gave us so much love and care.

He told the stories that shaped our days—

of family, faith, and the old-time ways.

Every moment felt gentle and free…

His life still guiding me.

Grandpa, your love, your stories, and your legacy will forever stay with me.

Thank you for all the memories.

TEACHERS' CORNER

📘 1. Reading Level & Classroom Use

Recommended Ages: 4–9 **Grade Levels:** K–3 **Reading Level:** Early Fluent Reader (Guided Reading Level J–L) **Lexile Estimate:** 480L–620L *(based on sentence structure, vocabulary, and narrative complexity)*

Why it fits K–3 classrooms

- Repetition and predictable phrasing support early readers.
- Rich vocabulary ("legacy," "democracy," "brilliance," "harvest," "tradition") supports 2nd–3rd grade comprehension.
- Strong SEL themes: identity, belonging, empathy, community responsibility, cultural pride.
- Rural life elements (trees, berry picking, old trucks, nature scenes) support science and social studies integration.
- Music, storytelling, and community traditions support arts integration.

2. Sight Word Lists

- Pre-K & Kindergarten High-Frequency Words
  the · and · you · we · with · then · when · his · can · like · look · here · said · are · my · me · they · he · she · do · go · to · in · is · it · on · up · at · so · of · hurt · still · berries · barber · drums · guitar · clapping · rapping

  Example: "My grandpa loves me, and I love him too."

- 1st Grade Sight Words

  every · where · give · takes · free · fun · day · wish · stay · calm · name · same · work · help · best · proud · stories · crowd · carry · people · together

  Example: "He keeps me calm when I see a snake."

  2nd–3rd Grade Vocabulary Builders

  legacy · brilliance · injustice · democracy · peaceful · graduation · education · competent · brilliant · history · community · volunteer · honors · encourage · tradition · heritage · resin · harvest · shade · distress · generation · responsibility · reunion · raspy · regal · bowlegged · awards · choose · gum tree / sweet-gum · veterinary / vet · marched · tambourines

  Example: "My Grandpa wants me to know my history, the brilliance of my legacy …"

💛 3. Social Emotional Learning (SEL) Connections

Self-Awareness

"Understanding personal identity through family stories and heritage. 'Grandpa showed us where we come from — and where we can go.'"

Self-Management

"Staying calm in new or scary situations. 'Don't worry, it won't hurt you … just stay still and calm.'"

Social Awareness

"Respecting elders, community helpers, and cultural traditions. 'Everyone in the community knows my grandpa by name … treats everyone the same.'"

Relationship Skills

- "Bonding with family, listening, helping, and showing appreciation.

  'He helps to feed people in need … mentors young people.'"

Responsible Decision-Making

- "Learning about voting, peaceful change, and community service. 'He marched peacefully to help bring change … took me to the voting booth.'"

Cultural Pride & Family Legacy

- Seeing oneself as part of a bigger story.
- Understanding that memories help keep loved ones close.
- Appreciating diversity within families and communities.

 ## 4. Comprehension & Discussion Questions (K–3)

Before Reading

- What do you think makes someone a hero?
- What special things do you do with your grandparents or family members?

During Reading

- How does Grandpa show love to his family?
- What does the child learn from spending time with Grandpa?
- Why does the community respect Grandpa so much?
- What do you notice about the rural setting (trees, berries, old truck)?

After Reading

- What lesson do you think Grandpa wants the children to remember?
- How does learning about history help us today?
- What is one way YOU can help your community like Grandpa?
- Why is it important to listen to stories from older generations?

 ## 5. Writing & Drawing Prompts

K–1 Prompts

- Draw a picture of you and someone in your family doing something fun.
- Finish the sentence: "My hero is ___ because."
- Draw the sweet-gum tree, berries, or Grandpa's truck from the story.

2nd–3rd Grade Prompts

- Write about a time when someone older taught you something important.
- Describe a tradition in your family and why it matters.
- Write a short paragraph about how you can help your community.
- Write about a place in nature that feels special to your family.

6. Curriculum Alignment (K–3)

English Language Arts (ELA)

- RL.K–3.1: Ask and answer questions about key details.
- RL.K–3.3: Describe characters, settings, and major events.
- RL.2–3.4: Determine meaning of words and phrases.
- RI.3.3: Describe relationships between historical events.

Social Studies

- Civics: Voting, community helpers, peaceful change.
- History: Family heritage, generational storytelling, civil rights.
- Geography: Rural life, travel, community spaces, nature exploration.

SEL Standards (CASEL)

- Self-Awareness
- Social Awareness
- Relationship Skills
- Responsible Decision-Making

Arts Integration

- Music appreciation (saxophone, drums, community performances).
- Oral storytelling traditions.
- Nature-inspired rhythm patterns.

AUTHORS NOTE TO THE CHILDREN

Dear Children

Thank you for reading my story. I wrote this book to share the love, wisdom, and joy my grandpa gave to me — and to remind you that your own family stories matter too.

Grandpas, grandmas, aunties, uncles, cousins, and caregivers all help shape who we become. They teach us lessons, tell us stories, and show us the kind of love that stays with us forever.

As you grow, I hope you will:

- listen to the stories in your family,
- ask questions about your history,
- be proud of where you come from, and
- carry kindness into your community.

Most of all, I hope you remember that **you are part of a beautiful legacy**, and your story is still being written every day.

With love,

Brenda G. Stanley

www.ingramcontent.com/pod-product-compliance
Lightning Source LLC
Chambersburg PA
CBHW041034120726
48005CB00005B/809